VICTORIAN LIFE

A VICTORIAN HOLIDAY

SHEILA WATSON

Wayland

VICTORIAN LIFE

A VICTORIAN CHRISTMAS

A VICTORIAN FACTORY

A VICTORIAN HOLIDAY

A VICTORIAN SCHOOL

A VICTORIAN STREET

A VICTORIAN SUNDAY

VICTORIAN CLOTHES

VICTORIAN TRANSPORT

HOW WE LEARN ABOUT THE VICTORIANS

Queen Victoria reigned from 1837 to 1901, a time when Britain went through enormous social and industrial changes. We can learn about Victorians in various ways. We can still see many of their buildings standing today, we can look at their documents, maps and artefacts – many of which can be found in museums. Photography, invented during Victoria's reign, gives us a good picture of life in Victorian Britain. In this book you will see what Victorian life was like through some of this historical evidence.

Series design: Pardoe Blacker Ltd
Editor: Sarah Doughty

First published in 1993 by Wayland (Publishers) Ltd
61 Western Road, Hove, East Sussex BN3 1JD, England

© Copyright 1993 Wayland (Publishers) Ltd

British Library Cataloguing in Publication Data
Watson, Sheila
    Victorian Holiday. - (Victorian Life Series)
    I. Title II. Series
    306. 480941

ISBN 0 7502 0719 1

Printed and bound in Great Britain by B.P.C.C Paulton Books Ltd

Cover picture: The seaside in late Victorian times.

Picture acknowledgements
Bass Museum, Bass Brewers, Burton 19 (top); Bridgeman Art Library cover, 8, 9 (bottom), 10 (bottom), 12, 20, 25 (top); E.T Archive 17 (top); Greg Evans Photo Library 27; Mary Evans Picture Library 7 (bottom), 9 (top), 10 (top), 11, 13 (top) and bottom (Fawcett Library), 14 (both), 17 (bottom), 23 (top); 24 (bottom), 26 (top); Great Yarmouth Central Library 25 (bottom); Hulton-Deutsch Collection 4, 7 (top), 15, 16, 21 (bottom), 26 (bottom); Illustrated London News Picture Library 6, 18, 21 (top); Billie Love Historical Collection 23 (bottom right); Oxfordshire Photographic Archive 5; Punch Picture Library 22; The Robert Opie Collection 23 (top right), 24 (top); Wayland Picture Library 19 (bottom).

CONTENTS

HOLIDAYS AT HOME

How many holidays do you have? Perhaps you spend part of them away with your family for a week or two each year. At the start of Queen Victoria's reign in 1837 only rich people had enough money to take holidays. Many poor people could not afford to have more than one day's holiday a year because they were only paid on the days they worked. They also did not earn enough money to travel very far.

THE FIRST HOLIDAYS

For many working people in 1837 the only days that were holidays were Sundays, and church holidays such as Easter. Others took a day's holiday for a special outing or event, such as when the fair came to their town or village. Some people went to fairs to enjoy themselves. Others went to find work and to buy and sell things. At early Victorian fairs people could watch dancing shows, boxing or wrestling matches. There were also simple amusements such as swings for two people.

Greenwich Fair, between 1800 and 1850.

The Victorians did not have coca-cola, sandwiches, hot-dogs or hamburgers as refreshments. Instead, they drank lemonade or beer and ate whelks, jellied eels, buns and brandy snaps.

St Giles's Fair, Oxford, 1885.

ENTERTAINMENTS

Towards the end of Victoria's reign there were many more entertainments at fairs. People could enjoy steam-driven rides such as the big wheel and the galloper with horses (a big roundabout). There were sideshows and often a display of animals or people with strange or unusually-shaped bodies. The Victorians called these displays 'freakshows'.

This picture of St Giles's Fair at Oxford shows they had a troupe of performing dogs and monkeys. Their marionette show would be made up of puppets worked by strings. A shooting range was another entertainment at the fair.

THE CHRISTMAS HOLIDAY

In England, Ireland and Wales Christmas Day was one of the few days nearly everyone had as a holiday and they made it a special day. Even those people who could not afford meat on other days tried to have beef or goose on Christmas Day, followed by plum pudding. Rich people often gave presents of food to the poor. Some poor people like this seamstress in her garret would not have anything special on Christmas Day.

In Scotland, rich and poor treated Christmas as an ordinary working day. They celebrated the New Year or Hogmanay with dances and feasts.

A seamstress in her garret on Christmas Day, 1877.

CHRISTMAS FOR THE WEALTHY

The picture at the top of the next page shows what it may have been like in a rich person's home on Christmas Day.

Rich people would have spent the day at home with their families. In England and Wales it became usual to give presents to family and friends on Christmas Day.

From 1870 onwards, rich children hung up stockings for Santa Claus or Father Christmas and found them filled with toys on Christmas morning.

A rich family opening presents.

HOLIDAYS WITH GUESTS

Rich people enjoyed entertaining their friends at holiday time. They sometimes asked friends to stay with them as guests in their country houses. Special activities were arranged for their visitors. In Scotland, they might be invited to shoot grouse in August. The guests in turn were expected to entertain their friends. Sometimes they put on plays or performed music.

Shooting grouse.

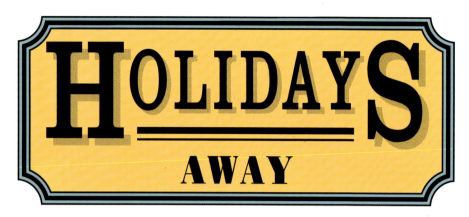

HOLIDAYS AWAY

In the early years of Victoria's reign few people could go far from their homes because travelling was so difficult. However, the growth of the railways during the 1840s changed the lives of people in Britain. People could save up and enjoy an annual holiday at a popular resort. Many more people took day trips or went away for a longer holiday.

THE PROBLEM OF TRAVELLING

In 1837, travel was expensive and difficult. Poor people usually walked everywhere. Some people used coaches and horses but this was uncomfortable and took a long time. Look at how many people want to climb on board this coach to Brighton. Travel was so difficult even for the rich

THE 3 BROWNS BOOK'D FOR BRIGHTON, AND ONLY ONE PLACE.

Journey to Brighton.

that very few people thought of travelling somewhere just to enjoy themselves. They went on holiday to improve their health or to educate themselves by visiting new places.

PLEASURE STEAMERS

Pleasure steamers took people on day trips along the river or around the coast. Steamers were one of the first popular ways of travelling at holiday time. People who could not afford to go away and stay somewhere on holiday could buy a ticket and go for a day trip on a pleasure steamer. This picture on the right shows an outing by steamer on the Thames.

A holiday trip down the Thames.

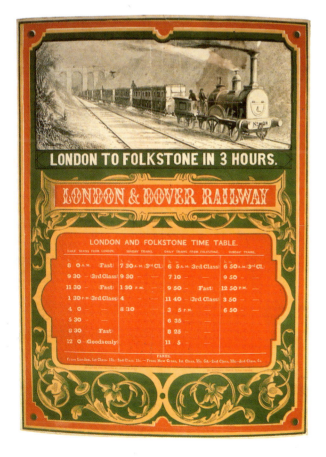

LONDON TO FOLKSTONE IN 3 HOURS.

LONDON & DOVER RAILWAY

LONDON AND FOLKSTONE TIME TABLE.

Railway timetable for the London and Dover railway.

THE RAILWAYS

By the end of the 1840s, Britain had built a wide railway network. Cheap railway fares meant that more and more people could travel long distances.

This early timetable shows the prices of tickets for trains that ran between London and Folkestone. The rich travelled first class and paid more for their tickets than second class travellers. Third class tickets were bought by poorer people. In 1844, a law made railways run at least one train per day for the third class (poorest) passengers.

THE TRAINS

At first, railways were not very comfortable for the third class passengers. Carriages like the one in this picture on the right were open to the cold, wind and rain. Even the first class carriages had no heating and in winter passengers had to bring their own blankets. There were no lavatories on most trains until the 1870s. All these discomforts did not stop people from travelling by train. Day trips or excursions became very popular.

Poster for an excursion by train, 1860s.

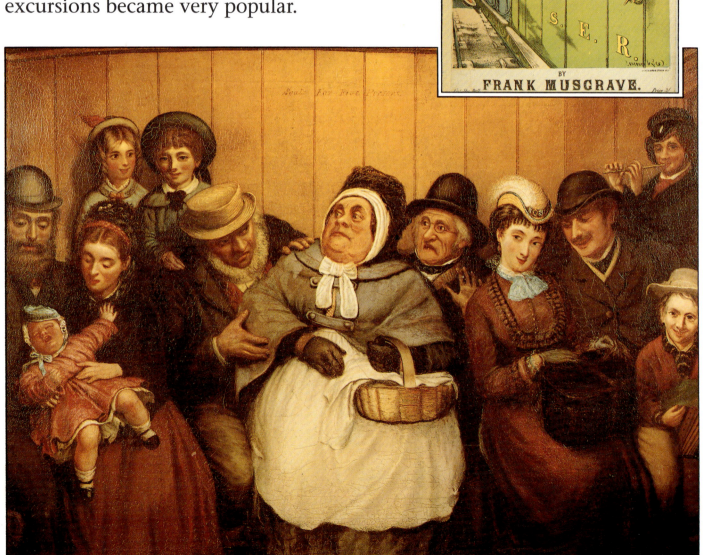

A crowded railway carriage.

RAILWAY CARRIAGES

Carriages such as the one on page 10 were often very crowded because travelling by train was so popular. The seat in the carriage is meant for only five people but is crammed full. People would use the railways to take them to holidays by the sea or in the country. Sometimes they would stay for a few weeks before returning by train.

Crowded horse-bus, 1851.

OTHER FORMS OF TRANSPORT

Other forms of transport were also used to go on trips or holidays. Once people reached their destinations by train they used horses and carriages to take them to their lodgings or to see the sights. Sometimes these forms of transport could be very crowded. Horse trams were used as early as 1845 in Southend. In 1885 Blackpool had the first electric street tram.

HOLIDAYS FOR THE RICH

Very rich, upper-class people had many more holidays than poor people and they could afford to spend a great deal more money enjoying themselves. When they went away they often took their servants with them. Middle-class people were able to afford several weeks' holiday a year.

Boating at Henley.

THE HENLEY REGATTA

Sporting events were very popular amongst all classes in Victorian times. Rich people often timed their holidays so they could go to these events. The picture above shows the Henley Regatta, a four-day boat race that was held every year in the first week of July. Racing at Ascot was another important event in the sporting calendar. In Scotland, deer stalking and grouse shooting were popular pastimes.

HOLIDAYS ABROAD

Cartoon of tourists at Vesuvius in Italy.

Only rich Victorians could afford to go abroad for their holidays. Some went to improve their health. Others went to educate themselves by visiting places with historical interest. Some looked for adventure, like these tourists climbing the volcano, Vesuvius in Italy shown in the picture above.

EXPLORATION

A few Victorians went abroad for several months or years. One brave woman, Mary Kingsley (1862-1900) travelled widely across west Africa and was the first European to enter parts of the continent. While she was there, she ate hippopotamus and crocodile.

Mary Kingsley.

A ROYAL PICNIC

During Victorian times people began to visit the countryside. They enjoyed walking and looking at the scenery. Wales, Scotland, the East Anglian Broads and the Lakeland district became very popular with Victorians. Queen Victoria helped to make Scottish holidays fashionable. This picture shows her eating luncheon in the Scottish highlands.

Queen Victoria at Cairn Lochan, 1861.

SEASIDE AMUSEMENTS

On holiday, Victorians liked to have something to keep them busy. They especially enjoyed learning something new. In this picture you can see how middle-class Victorian girls passed the time at the seaside.

Some are looking for shells on the seashore. Others are searching for rocks and fossils with hammers. Some are sketching the scenery. What other activities are they doing?

Middle-class girls at the seaside.

FASHIONABLE RESORTS

Some rich people chose their holiday resort because it was a fashionable place to go to. They wanted to make sure that they would meet people of the same class as themselves. This picture shows the famous Esplanade area of the Isle of Wight in about 1900, a place where many middle-class people would spend their holidays. It remained fashionable until long after Victoria died.

The Isle of Wight, in the early years of this century.

HOLIDAYS FOR THE POOR

At the beginning of Victoria's reign many people worked long hours six days a week. They did not have much spare time or money to spend on holidays. After 1850 it became more common for working people to have Saturday afternoons off. In 1871, bank holidays were introduced. By the end of Victoria's reign many working people had more holidays than they had in 1837 and more money to spend.

DAY TRIPS TO SPECIAL EVENTS

Until the 1850s most working people did not go away from home for more than one day every year. They might go to special events such as the Great Exhibition of 1851 at Hyde Park. The railways offered people special excursion tickets to visit the Exhibition. This meant that many people who lived outside London could make a day trip in to the city. Once in London people used horse-drawn transport like this to reach the Exhibition.

Going to the Exhibition, 1851.

SPORTING EVENTS

Throughout Victoria's reign all types of people enjoyed a day's holiday at the races. For many it was a good place to meet people and show off the latest fashions.

As time went on more and more people enjoyed watching or taking part in sport. For example, the Football Association Cup was started in 1871. All the football clubs were invited to help buy a Cup to be played for by all the clubs.

Women began to play more sport such as lawn tennis which became popular during the 1870s.

The Derby Day.

BANK HOLIDAYS

These people in the picture on the right are watching the lions being fed at London zoo on a bank holiday. The first bank holiday was in 1871. The banker, Sir John Lubbock had led a campaign to introduce bank holidays, and at first only the banks closed on that day. By the end of Victoria's reign shops and factories also began to close on bank holidays.

Feeding the lions at Regent's Park.

A DAY'S OUTING

Holidaymakers on
Hampstead Heath.

People liked to spend a day's holiday visiting
museums or parks. Hampstead Heath was a
favourite place for Londoners to go on fine
days, and thousands of people would flock
there. Some would take a picnic. Picnics
became very fashionable in Victoria's reign
because the Queen herself enjoyed them so
much. Other people hired donkeys or ponies
for short rides. Churches sometimes organized
special outings for choirs or members of the
Sunday school. Children often had organized
games and a picnic tea.

THE WORKERS' OUTING

Towards the end of Victoria's reign factories began to organize special day trips for their workers. Here on the right is a poster for a Bass Brewery workers' outing to Great Yarmouth in Norfolk. The whole workforce came to Yarmouth for the day from Burton-on-Trent in the Midlands. Fifteen trains were used. The first train left Burton at 3.50 am and the last train arrived back home at 2.35 the next morning. The Brewery paid for all the entertainments at the seaside resort.

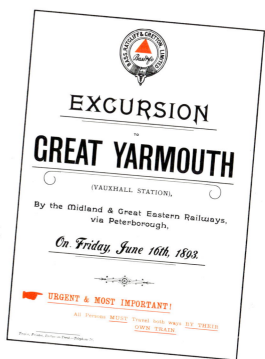

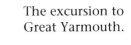

The excursion to Great Yarmouth.

Queen Victoria's Jubilee festival at Wakefield.

THE QUEEN'S JUBILEE

In 1887, Queen Victoria celebrated fifty years on the throne. Special events were organized all over the country to celebrate her Jubilee, like this festival at Wakefield. In recent times people have celebrated events such as royal weddings in the same way with parades and parties.

SEASIDE HOLIDAYS

Do you enjoy going to the seaside? Many Victorians loved going to visit the seaside resorts. Queen Victoria used to take her children for holidays on the Isle of Wight. Victorian children were given the chance to run and play in the open air, paddle in the water and build sandcastles.

An early seaside resort.

EARLY SEASIDE RESORTS

This picture shows an early beach scene at Rottingdean. Seaside holidays were not so popular then as they were to become in late Victorian times. You can see there are some people on the beach, including fishermen with their boats, but there are few of the attractions that would later bring people flocking to the seaside.

THE SEA FOR HEALTH

To begin with, most visitors came to the seaside
to try and improve their health. The seaside
remained a favourite place for invalids
to come and take in the sea air.
Victorians thought that drinking
seawater was good for them. Children
sometimes had to begin each day of
their holidays by gulping down a
glass of seawater.

Invalid in a wheelchair.

At first people did not swim in the
sea for pleasure. They went into the
sea in the early morning when it was
quite cold and only dipped their
bodies in it. They thought this was better for
them than going in the sea later in the day
when it was warmer.

THE SEASIDE RESORTS

At first only rich people could
afford to go on seaside holidays.
They rented a house or apartment
and took their own servants to look
after them. By the 1860s hotels had
been built in most seaside resorts.
Brighton was one of the first
popular and fashionable resorts.

Brighton
seafront,
1890s.

LODGING HOUSES

Those who could not afford to stay in hotels stayed in lodgings. Sometimes their rooms were small and crowded like the one illustrated in this cartoon below. Food was bought by the visitors and cooked by the landlady. There were many complaints about how bad the cooking was and how some landladies ate their visitors' food themselves.

A cartoon showing a crowded lodging house, from *Punch*.

CROWDED STATE OF LODGING HOUSES

Lodging-House Keeper. "On'y this room to let, mem. A four-post—a tent,—and a very comfortable double-bedded chest of drawers for the young gentlemen."

DRESSING FOR THE BEACH

People dressed up to go to the beach. Even poor families would try to wear new clothes. Women had special dresses made in the latest fashions. Men, women and children all wore hats, and often gloves too. Women carried umbrellas or parasols to shade their faces from the sun. A suntan was very unfashionable and the sun and wind thought to be harmful to the skin. Even when they went into the sea people wore clothes which covered most of their bodies.

Beach clothes.

HOLIDAY SOUVENIRS

What sort of souvenirs do you bring back from holiday? Victorians collected shells, rocks and seaweed. They also bought useful items, often which had the name or picture of the place they had visited. Jewellery boxes, ink stands, candle holders, jugs and plates were bought and taken home. Later in Victoria's reign, photographs became popular souvenirs.

Useful souvenirs from holiday resorts.

BEACH VISITS

Victorians had many rules about how to behave on the beach. People were supposed to be properly dressed when they were at the seaside. When swimming for pleasure became popular, men and women were not supposed to swim together. They had to swim at different times or in different parts of the beach.

Dipping into the sea from a bathing-machine.

BATHING-MACHINES

The Victorians did not like other people to see them when their bathing clothes were wet and clung to their bodies. They had bathing-machines which were large huts on wheels dragged in and out of the water by horses. People changed inside them and then used the steps at the front to climb in and out of the water.

ON THE BEACH

At the top of the next page is a picture of a beach in 1864. In the picture you can see people riding donkeys, others out strolling and children playing in the sand. There is a row of bathing-machines in the distance.

The beach at Weston Sands, 1864.

THE LATE VICTORIAN SEASIDE

Below is a photograph of Yarmouth beach in 1895. It is later in Victoria's reign than the picture above, but the clothes are still formal. Men still wear hats. The women still wear gloves and carry parasols. There are bathing-machines in the background. Look at the metal chairs people sat on. They have not yet been replaced by deck chairs. The boats are for taking visitors on sea trips. You can see how few people there are swimming in the sea.

Yarmouth beach, 1895.

BEACH ENTERTAINMENTS

There were many entertainments on the beach at busy times of the day. This picture shows a Punch and Judy show for the children and Minstrels, who dressed up in costumes and danced and sang to entertain holidaymakers. Near the beach you would find funfairs, bandstands, a boating lake and gardens. What sort of entertainments do you find on or near the beach today?

At the seaside, 1870s.

The Victorians built large constructions out of cast iron such as piers, towers and big wheels, to entertain holidaymakers. In this picture below is Blackpool Tower. From here visitors could see for miles. Each year, visitors came to Blackpool from the industrial towns of Yorkshire and Lancashire. They had a little money in their pockets and they wished to spend it. Blackpool developed a funfair with entertainments such as the Ferris wheel and the roller coaster.

Blackpool, 1903.

A BEACH TODAY

The beach at Scarborough in Yorkshire today.

At first sight a beach holiday today looks very different from the ones the Victorians enjoyed. People wear fewer clothes on the beach. However, they still enjoy the same entertainments as the Victorians.

They build sandcastles, paddle and swim in the sea. They eat shrimps and cockles. They have donkey rides. The Victorians invented the seaside holiday as we know it. How far has it really changed?

TIME LINE

BC   AD 0   500

43   410

                          'THE DARK AGES'

ROMAN   ANGLO-SAXONS
BRITAIN

CELTS   VIKINGS

EARLY YEARS

1730s First recorded bathing-machines at Scarborough.

1784 First mail coach service.

1812 Henry Bell of Glasgow began Britain's first passenger steamer service with the ship *Comet* on the Clyde.

1813 First steam pleasure boats on the Thames.

1820s

Iron was used to build piers at seaside towns.

Regular steam ferry trips between Calais and Dover.

1825 Stockton to Darlington steam railway opened for passengers.

1830s

1830 Railway line built between Manchester and Liverpool.

1837 Victoria became Queen.

1840s

1841 Brighton was the first major seaside town to have a railway.

1844 A law made all railway companies provide seats for third class passengers. Price set at 1d (one old penny) a mile. Carriages had to be closed and waterproof.

1841 Thomas Cook, a Baptist lay preacher, organized his first train excursion to Loughborough for his congregation. This was the start of a tour business.

1845 Horse-tram used on Southend pier.

1850s

Growth in the number of public museums and art galleries from 59 before 1850 to 295 by 1914.

1850 Factory Act. Textile factory workers had to have Saturday afternoon off as well as Sunday each week.

1851 Great Exhibition at Hyde Park, London.

1860s

Rapid growth in hotel building.

1865 First horse-drawn street tram (Portsmouth).

1870s

1871 First bank holiday.

FA (Football Association) competition started.

1873 County cricket championship formed.

1874 Lawn tennis began to become popular.

1874 The Midland Railway Company imported a few Pullman carriages from America which had lavatory compartments.

1880s

Deck chairs made of canvas and wood began to replace chairs made of iron and wood at the seaside.

The beginning of holidays with pay for a few workers.

1883 Electric railway operated along the seafront at Brighton.

1885 First electric street tramway in England in Blackpool.

1888 Football League founded.

1890s

1894 Post Office gave up its monopoly (sole right to sell) of stamped postcards. Beginning of the holiday postcard.

1885 Most railway carriages had lavatories.

1900s

1901 Queen Victoria died.

1902 It became legal for messages as well as addresses to be written on the backs of cards.

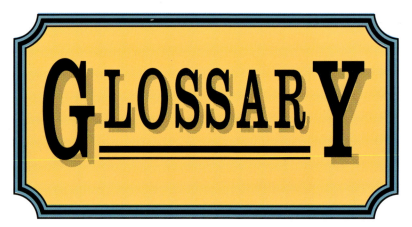

GLOSSARY

Apartment A set of rooms rented for a holiday.

Bathing-machine A wooden hut on wheels, drawn into the sea by a horse. Victorians changed their clothes inside bathing-machines before and after going into the water.

Deer stalking Hunting and killing deer for sport.

Destination The place someone or something is travelling to.

Excursion A short outward and return journey, usually for a day's holiday.

Fossils Rocks which have taken on the shapes of long dead plants, shells or animals.

Freakshow A word used by Victorians to describe a display of people or animals with unusual shapes at circuses or fairs.

Great Exhibition The displays of crafts and industries held in one large building in Hyde Park, London, in 1851.

Grouse A type of bird. Grouse are shot for sport and food.

Invalid A person who is sick or not able-bodied.

Jubilee A special anniversary or celebration, usually for a monarch after twenty-five or fifty years on the throne.

Landlady A woman who rents out rooms to visitors.

Lodgings Places where people stay that are usually cheaper than hotels.

Minstrels Travelling entertainers who made music.

Parasol A light umbrella used to keep sun off the face.

Piers Platforms raised above the sea by wooden or iron supports. Many had entertainments on them.

Pleasure steamer A boat, powered by steam, which took people on day trips up and down rivers or along the coast.

Resort A place where people go on holiday, usually at the seaside.

Tram A carriage which runs on tracks like trains do. Used in towns to carry people short distances.

Whelk A sea creature with a snail-like shell.

BOOKS TO READ

Aylett, J. A *Century of Change: Twentieth Century Holidays* (Hodder and Stoughton, 1989)
Bentley, D. *Christmas* (Wayland, 1988)
Bild, I. and Humphries, S. *Finding Out About Seaside Holidays* (Batsford Academic and Educational Ltd, 1983)
Ross, S. *Our Holidays* (Wayland, 1992)
Siliprandi, K. *A Victorian Christmas* (Wayland, 1992)
Wood, T. *At the Seaside* (A & C Black, 1992)

PLACES TO VISIT

Many museums have displays on Victorian transport, leisure and entertainments. The following is a small selection.

ENGLAND

Avon: Weston-super-Mare: Woodspring Museum, Burlington Street, BS23 1PR. Tel. 0934 621028
Dorset: Time Walk Museum, Brewers' Quay, Hope Square, Weymouth, DN4 8NF. Tel. 0305 777622
Kent: Ramsgate Museum, Ramsgate Library, Guildford Lawn, Ramsgate, CT11 9AY. Tel. 0843 593532
Lancashire: Liverpool Museum, William Brown Street, Liverpool, L3 8EN. Tel. 051 207 0001
London: Bethnal Green Museum of Childhood, Cambridge Heath Road, E2 9PA. Tel. 081 980 4315
London Transport Museum, Covent Garden, WC2E 7BB. Tel. 071 379 6344
Norfolk: Bressingham Steam Museum, Bressingham, Diss, IP22 2AB. Tel. 0379 88386
Cromer Museum, East Cottages, Tucker Street, Cromer, NR27 9HS. Tel. 0263 513543
Tolhouse Museum, Tolhouse Street, Great Yarmouth, NR30 2SQ. Tel. 0493 858900
Yorkshire: National Railway Museum, Leeman Road, York, YO2 4XJ. Tel. 0904 621261

The Rotunda Museum of Archaeology and Local History, Museum Terrace, Vernon Road, Scarborough, YO11 2PW. Tel. 0723 374839

SCOTLAND

Broughty Castle Museum, Broughty Ferry, Dundee, DD5 2BE. Tel. 0382 76121
Museum of Childhood, 42 High Street, Edinburgh, Lothian, EH1 1TG. Tel. 031 225 2424
Museum of Transport, Kelvin Hall, 1 Bunhouse Road, Glasgow, G3 8PZ. Tel. 041 357 3929

WALES

Clwyd: Rhyl Library, Museum and Arts Centre, Church Street, Rhyl, LL18 3AA. Tel. 0745 353814

NORTHERN IRELAND

Ulster: Ulster Folk and Transport Museum, Witham Street Gallery, Newtownards Road, Belfast, BT4 1HP. Tel. 0232 451519

INDEX